Let your travel destinations and activities inspire easy DIY jewelry!

Wanderlust

LEISURE ARTS, INC. • Maumelle, Arkansas

Meet the Designer

Lena Prima's jewelry designs reflect her life as a singer, recording artist, songwriter, artist, author, and world traveler. She is the youngest daughter of music legend Louis Prima and classically trained singer Gia Maione Prima. During his five-decade career, her dad's mega-hit songs included "Jump, Jive and Wail," "Just a Gigolo," "I Wanna Be Like You" (written for the King Louis orangutan in Disney's The Jungle Book), "That Old Black Magic," and others.

Lena grew up in the exciting cities of Las Vegas and New Orleans (her father's hometown). She spent much of her childhood on stage singing, dancing, and touring with her parents. Since 1991, Lena has had a full-time singing career, doing shows in Las Vegas, New Orleans, and throughout the country. She has recorded four highly acclaimed albums and resides in New Orleans, performing regularly at the historic Hotel Monteleone (where her dad also performed).

Lena Prima

Lena's Musical Legacy

Lena adored the sheer joy of her father's raucous swing as well as the rock and funk artists she loved listening to as a teenager. Her recordings and her show reflect all these influences, featuring her own wonderful songs, beautiful ballads, jazz standards, rock and roll, and, of course, a healthy dose of her father's hits. Over the years Lena's show has grown into a rousing, highly acclaimed celebration of her musical roots as well as her musical journey.

For a taste of Lena's music, download her albums at lenaprima.com. Her concerts may be tracked at bandsintown.com/lenaprima.

Not content to limit her creative outlet to music alone, Lena is a respected and prolific artist and jewelry designer. She began her own line of jewelry, "Pennies From Heaven," in 2006, creating bracelets with a tiny penny to commemorate her favorite childhood memory of her father and his famous song by that name. She has also taught jewelry classes and enjoys making special pieces to wear on her travels.

Lena also hopes to help people find creative ways of using the many beautiful jewelry elements found in craft stores. "It is very overwhelming to just see all those pieces in the store and hard to know what to do with them," she says. "I hope this book will inspire you to make your own jewelry and to go have some travel adventures as well!"

The unique pieces in this book were created to capture the charm of favorite places and events from Lena's personal and professional travels as a singer and artist.

"Whenever I am traveling, I like to make jewelry to take with me that I can mix and match and that will always remind me of that particular trip," she says. "I like jewelry that is easy to make so I can put something together quickly."

This collection is designed to be made using only two tools and basically just opening and closing jump rings.

With a pair of chain-nose pliers on each side of the jump ring, open the jump ring by pulling one pair of pliers toward you while pushing the other away ***(Fig. A)*.**

Close the jump ring by pushing and pulling the pliers in opposite directions, bringing the ring ends back together.

You'll also open and close the loops on ear wires the same way.

Fig. A

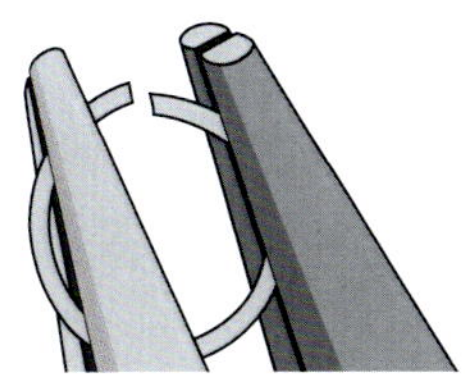

Seaside Memories

"I love beaches and have been to many all over the country and the Caribbean. I enjoy having an elegant seaside jewelry set to wear out to dinner with a nice tan after a day at the beach. I love the sparkles in the charms of this set (page 5), reminding me of the shimmer in the sand and on the water. The pearl earrings from the Dreaming of Paris set (page 27) can also be worn with this set.

"The Pacific Coast Highway is such a breathtaking drive, with the blue of the ocean and the majestic rocks and cliffs. These stones (page 6) remind me of the ones I gathered on the beach at Patrick's Point State Park. The necklace is designed to go over your head and can be worn alone casual or dressed up with the bracelet and earrings from the New York City set (page 30)."

—Lena Prima

Sparkling Sand

NECKLACE SHOPPING LIST

- ☐ 24" long silver hammered circle chain
- ☐ 2 silver ocean-themed charms
- ☐ large silver seashell pendant
- ☐ 4 bead, rhinestone, and pearl bead dangles
- ☐ large silver lobster clasp
- ☐ 12mm silver jump ring
- ☐ 6mm silver jump rings
- ☐ chain-nose pliers (2 pair)

Finished necklace length: approximately 16 1/2"

Necklace

1. Separate chain into three 8" pieces; set one length aside for bracelet.
2. Use large jump ring to attach one end of each chain to the pendant.
3. Use a small jump ring to attach the lobster clasp to end of one chain.
4. Use small jump rings to attach charms to the necklace two links above the pendant. Attach the bead dangles to the necklace on either side of the charms.

Bracelet

Make a coordinating bracelet using the remaining chain from the necklace. Use an 8mm jump ring to attach a lobster clasp to one end. Remove circles from chain to make bracelet desired length. Use an 8mm jump ring to attach a compass charm and an anchor charm to the opposite end.

Earrings

For coordinating earrings, use 6mm jump rings to attach anchor-themed charms to ear wires.

Pacific Coast Highway

NECKLACE SHOPPING LIST

- ☐ strand of 5 flat stone beads with attached large jump rings (about 12" long)
- ☐ four $^{7}/_{8}$" diameter hammered silver rings
- ☐ $11^{1}/_{2}$" long silver heavy hammered chain
- ☐ chain-nose pliers (2 pair)

Finished necklace length: approximately 26"

Necklace

1. Separate the stone strand, leaving a large jump ring attached to each side of each stone.
2. Join the stones together with a large hammered ring between each pair of large jump rings.
3. Attach the chain to the jump rings on each end of the stone strand.

New York City Bracelet and Earrings, page 30.

Music Festival

"I love performing at music festivals and the fashion trends that go along with them. The Edgy Rocker set (page 9) is for the rocker chick— faded torn jeans and boots, leather vests, and vintage rocker tees. This can also be worn with dressy, edgy outfits all year round. This is the set I would wear the most!

"The Boho set (page 12) is for the flower girl sort of vibe — maxi dresses and flowing kimonos. The necklace can be worn long or wrapped around twice. The harmonica bag charm (page 13) is a nice extra for your cross body purse."

—Lena Prima

Edgy Rocker

NECKLACE
SHOPPING LIST

- ☐ 30" long black chain with extension chain and clasp
- ☐ 28" long gunmetal fine chain necklace with attached rhinestone heart pendant, rhinestone bow charm, and black tassel
- ☐ 1 7/16" diameter "Music Makes My World Go Round" pendant (comes with attached harmonica charm)
- ☐ 7mm brass jump ring
- ☐ chain-nose pliers (2 pair)

Finished necklace length: approximately 30" excluding pendant and tassel

Necklace

1. Remove the harmonica charm from the pendant. Set the charm aside for another use.
2. Use the jump ring to attach the "Music Makes My World Go Round" pendant to the black chain.
3. Remove the tassel, heart, and bow from the remaining necklace. Set the necklace, heart, and bow aside to make the necklace and bracelet on page 10.
4. Attach the tassel to the pendant.

Earrings

Turn tassel pendants into matching earrings. Simply remove the bails and use 6mm jump rings to attach the tassels to ear wires.

If music's not your thing, make it your own!

Edgy Rocker

NECKLACE AND BRACELET SHOPPING LIST

- ☐ 20" long gunmetal heavy chain
- ☐ 26" long silver chain with extension chain
- ☐ 28" long gunmetal fine chain necklace with attached rhinestone heart pendant, rhinestone bow charm, and black tassel
- ☐ "Go Your Own Way" charm (ours was attached to an arrow pendant, used on page 19)
- ☐ 5mm brass jump ring
- ☐ 6mm silver jump rings
- ☐ 6mm gunmetal jump rings
- ☐ 6mm black jump rings
- ☐ 8mm silver jump rings
- ☐ 12mm silver jump ring
- ☐ small black lobster clasp
- ☐ large silver lobster clasp
- ☐ chain-nose pliers (2 pair)

Finished necklace length: approximately 28"
Finished bracelet length: approximately 8"

Necklace

1. Remove a 13" length from the gunmetal heavy chain. Set the remaining chain aside to use for the bracelet, below. Use 6mm gunmetal jump rings to attach the heavy chain 4" from each end of the silver chain (excluding the extension chain).
2. Attach an 8mm silver jump ring at the point where the extension chain is attached to the silver chain. Attach an 8mm silver jump ring at the opposite end of the silver chain.
3. Remove the rhinestone heart pendant, rhinestone bow charm, and tassel from the gunmetal fine chain. Set the tassel aside to make the necklace, page 8. Use a 6mm gunmetal jump ring to attach the gunmetal fine chain to each 8mm jump ring on the silver chain.
4. Attach the large lobster clasp to the 8mm silver jump ring on the end opposite the extension chain.
5. Remove the "Go Your Own Way" charm from the arrow pendant. Set the arrow pendant aside for another use.
6. Use a 5mm brass jump ring to attach the charm to the bottom of the heart pendant. Use a 12mm jump ring to attach the heart pendant to the gunmetal thick chain.

Bracelet

1. Separate the gunmetal heavy chain left over from the necklace into two equal pieces.
2. Attach an 8mm silver jump ring to the bar on each side of the rhinestone bow.
3. Use a 6mm silver jump ring to attach one end of the chain to one 8mm jump ring. Repeat for the remaining chain piece.
4. Use a 6mm black jump ring to attach the black lobster clasp to one chain end. Attach another 6mm black jump ring to the remaining chain end.

Boho

NECKLACE SHOPPING LIST

- ☐ 48" brown cord and pearl necklace with extension chain and lobster clasp
- ☐ 8 yellow, 7 grey, 7 peach, and 7 green flower charms with attached jump rings
- ☐ chain-nose pliers (2 pair)

Finished necklace length: 48" when worn long or approximately 24" when doubled around the neck.

Necklace

1. Beginning at one end of the necklace, use the attached jump ring to attach one yellow flower charm to the cord running alongside the first pearl on the necklace. Attach a grey flower charm to the next pearl. Attach a peach flower charm to the next pearl. Attach a green flower charm to the next pearl.
2. Repeating the sequence in Step 1, add the remaining flower charms to the necklace, ending with a yellow flower charm.

BAG CHARM SHOPPING LIST

- ☐ harmonica charm (ours was attached to the "Music Makes My World Go Round" pendant used on page 8)
- ☐ 12mm silver jump ring
- ☐ large silver lobster clasp
- ☐ chain-nose pliers (2 pair)

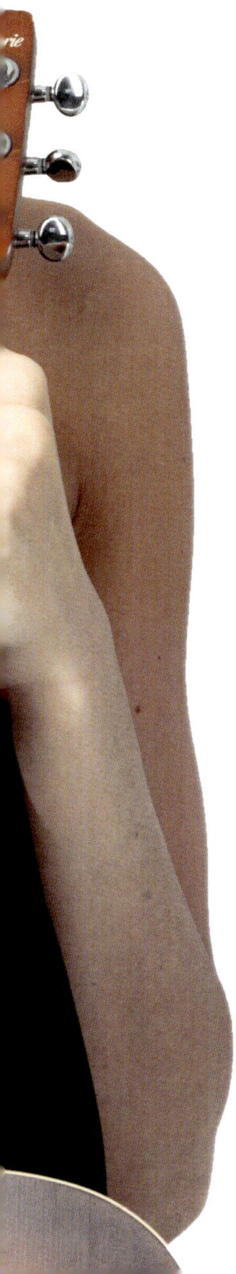

Bag Charm

1. Remove the harmonica charm from the pendant. Set the pendant aside for another use.
2. Use the jump ring to attach the lobster clasp to the harmonica charm.

Boho

BRACELET SHOPPING LIST

- ☐ two $1^{1}/_{4}$" diameter peach flower charms with filigree petals
- ☐ 24" long brass chain with decorative oval loops
- ☐ 6mm brass jump rings
- ☐ small brass lobster clasp with attached jump ring
- ☐ chain-nose pliers (2 pair)

Bracelet

1. Remove two oval loops from the chain.
2. Use jump rings to attach one oval loop and two charms together.
3. Attach the remaining oval loop and clasp together.
4. Measure the length of the joined charms and the length of the oval loop and clasp. Add these measurements together.
5. Subtract the measurement determined in Step 4 from the desired finished bracelet length. Remove the determined amount of chain. Separate this chain into two equal pieces.
6. Attach the lobster clasp to one end of one chain length. Attach the opposite end of the chain length to one flower charm.
7. Attach the remaining chain length to the remaining flower charm. Attach the oval loop to the remaining end of the chain.

Earrings

Create matching earrings by using 6mm brass jump rings to attach blue flower charms to ear wires.

Road Trip

"I loved Route 66 road trips and memories of the souvenir shops, trading posts and old-fashioned motel signs. As a young girl I loved rock collections, turquoise, coins and good luck charms. The three American West Necklaces (page 17) can be layered or worn individually. The turquoise bag charm (page 17) will look great on your leather travel bag.

"The New England Weekend set (page 21) is inspired by driving along the East Coast in the fall. Beautiful colors of all the leaves changing and dancing in the wind as they fall, a nice memory to relive every autumn when you wear them. I love how light this set is, just like the real leaves."

—Lena Prima

The American West

NECKLACE SET SHOPPING LIST

- ☐ 30" long silver chain with extension chain and matching clasp
- ☐ 27" long brass chain with extension chain and matching clasp
- ☐ 24" long gold chain with extension chain and matching clasp
- ☐ silver thunderbird charm
- ☐ turquoise drop, silver wing, and coin pendant
- ☐ silver and turquoise charm
- ☐ 5mm brass jump ring
- ☐ 5mm silver jump ring
- ☐ 5mm antique silver jump ring
- ☐ chain-nose pliers (2 pair)

Finished necklace lengths: approximately 30", 27" and 24", excluding pendants

Necklace Set

1. For the thunderbird charm necklace, use the antique silver jump ring to attach the thunderbird charm to the 30" chain.
2. For the turquoise drop and silver wing charm necklace, remove the coin charm from the turquoise drop, silver wing, and coin pendant. Set the coin charm aside to use on the necklace, page 18. Use the brass jump ring to attach the turquoise drop and silver wing to the 27" chain.
3. For the turquoise charm necklace, use the silver jump ring to attach the silver and turquoise charm to the 24" chain.

Bag Charm

Dress up your travel bag with a dangly charm. Use a 6mm jump ring to attach a silver and turquoise charm to a 12mm jump ring. Attach the large jump ring to a large lobster clasp.

Earrings

For each earring, join a 5mm silver jump ring and a 6mm silver jump ring together. Attach a silver and turquoise charm to the larger jump ring and an ear wire to the smaller jump ring.

Bracelet

Finished bracelet length: approximately 8"

Note: *We were able to buy the turquoise connectors in a strand of four.*

Attach two 8mm jump rings together to the end of the turquoise connector strand. Add two more jump rings together to the previous rings. Add 1 jump ring to these two rings.

Repeat for the remaining end of the strand, using a single ring at the end to attach a large silver lobster clasp.

ta Cruz
IFORNIA
HERE!

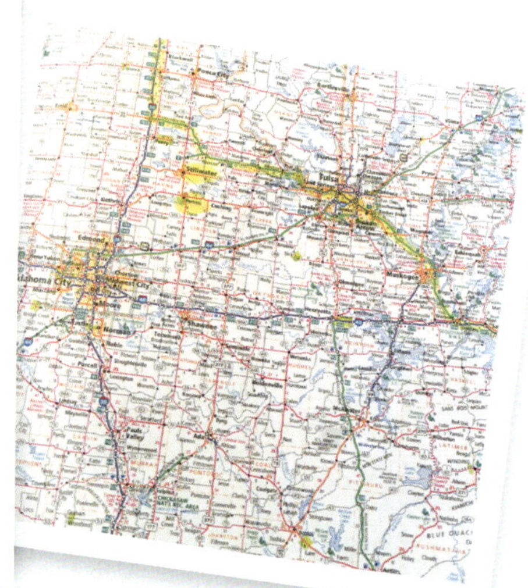

The American West

NECKLACE SHOPPING LIST

- ☐ 30" long brass chain with extension chain and matching clasp
- ☐ arrow pendant (ours was attached to the "Go Your Own Way" charm, used on page 10)
- ☐ coin pendant (ours was attached to the turquoise drop, silver wing, and coin pendant, used on page 16)
- ☐ brass triangle charm
- ☐ 6mm brass jump rings
- ☐ 3mm brass jump rings
- ☐ chain-nose pliers (2 pair)

Finished necklace length: approximately 18", excluding pendant

Necklace

1. Remove the charm from the arrow pendant. Set the charm aside for another use.
2. Separate the chain into three 10" pieces (excluding clasp and extension chain).
3. Use 6mm brass jump rings to attach the chain with the clasp to one side of the arrow pendant and to attach the chain with the extension chain to the other side of the arrow pendant.
4. Use a 6mm jump ring to attach the triangle charm to the arrow pendant.
5. Use 3mm jump rings to attach the remaining 10" length of chain 3" from the clasp and extension chain.
6. Remove the coin charm from the turquoise drop, silver wing, and coin pendant. Set the turquoise drop and silver wing charms aside for the necklace, page 16. Using a 6mm jump ring, attach the coin charm to the chain.

Earrings

For each earring, use two 5mm jump rings to attach one coin charm to an ear wire.

New England Weekend

NECKLACE SHOPPING LIST

- ☐ 24" long brass chain with decorative oval loops
- ☐ two 14" brass leaf and bead strands
- ☐ small brass lobster clasp
- ☐ 7mm brass jump rings
- ☐ 4mm brass jump rings
- ☐ chain-nose pliers (2 pair)

Finished necklace length: approximately 18"
Finished bracelet length: approximately 8"

Necklace

1. Beginning and ending with an oval loop, remove an 18" length of chain; set the remaining chain aside for the bracelet.
2. Use a 7mm jump ring to attach a lobster clasp to one end of the chain.
3. Separate the leaves and the bead strands.
4. Attach one leaf to a 4-bead strand. Use a 7mm jump ring to attach the bead strand to the center of the necklace.
5. Attach one leaf to a 3-bead strand. Repeat to make a total of two. Use a 4mm jump ring to attach one strand to each of the oval loops next to the center.
6. Attach one leaf to a 2-bead strand. Repeat to make a total of two. Use a 7mm jump ring to attach one strand to the center of each of the chain links next to the oval loop.

Bracelet and Earrings

Use the remaining chain, a leftover leaf, and leftover beads to make a beautiful bracelet and earrings. Use a 4mm jump ring to attach a 4-bead strand to each end of the leaf. Attach one oval loop (from the remaining chain) to one end of the bracelet. Use a 7mm jump ring to attach a small lobster clasp to the remaining end of the bracelet.

To make each earring, attach one leaf to a single-bead strand. Use a 7mm jump ring to attach the bead strand to an ear wire.

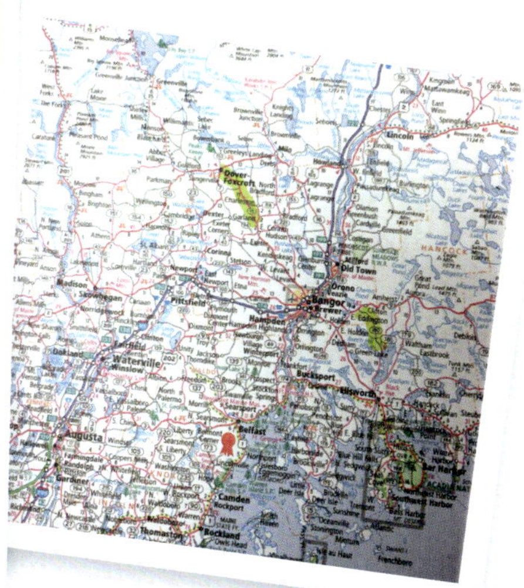
Lincoln
Dover-Foxcroft
Old Town
Orono
Bangor
Brewer
Hampden
Newport
Pittsfield
Madison
Skowhegan
Waterville
Winslow
Augusta
Gardiner
Bucksport
Ellsworth
Searsport
Belfast
Camden
Rockport
Rockland
Thomaston

City Girl

"My best friend and I are enamored with Paris, and we are constantly giving each other Eiffel Tower jewelry and accessories. I imagined us wearing these Dreaming of Paris pieces (pages 23-27) on a trip to Paris with black-and-white striped shirts and going to cafes, restaurants and shops. The necklace can be worn layered 4 different ways (pages 24-25), and the camera charm will look so cute on your clutch purse.

"I love the Sex and the City movie and television series, so the New York City set (page 28) is inspired by the four friends and can be worn dressed up or down, day or night. The "Love" necklace (page 31) is inspired by the keychain from the movie."

—Lena Prima

Dreaming of Paris

Earrings
For each earring, use a jump ring to attach a pink flower charm to an oval gemstone connector. Attach a silver ear wire to the opposite end of the connector.

Dreaming of Paris

NECKLACE SHOPPING LIST

- ☐ 24" long 10mm pearl and silver link chain
- ☐ 22" long 10mm pearl and silver link double-chain
- ☐ 20" long 10mm pearl necklace
- ☐ 18" long grey 8mm faceted bead and gunmetal chain
- ☐ five assorted Paris-themed charms
- ☐ $^{7}/_{8}$" x 1" oval gemstone and gunmetal connector
- ☐ $^{3}/_{4}$" pink flower charm
- ☐ silver extension chain
- ☐ large silver lobster clasp
- ☐ 2 small silver lobster clasps
- ☐ 2 small gunmetal lobster clasps
- ☐ 12mm silver jump rings, 8mm silver jump rings, and 6mm silver jump rings
- ☐ 6mm gunmetal jump rings
- ☐ chain-nose pliers (2 pair)

Finished necklace length: approximately 23", excluding the extension chain

Get four different looks from one necklace! The gunmetal chain and the pearl strand can be removed from the layered necklace for a more casual look or added on those days that you want a little more "bling!" The pieces can even be worn separately for a simple, classic look. And use some of the supplies remaining from your necklace to make a coordinating bracelet!

Necklace

1. Remove one pearl and double-chain length from each end of the chain. Set these aside to make the bracelet, page 27.
2. On one end of the chain, attach one 6mm, then one 8mm jump ring. Use another 6mm jump ring to attach the large lobster clasp to the 8mm jump ring. On the remaining end of the necklace, attach one 6mm, then one 8mm jump ring. Use another 6mm jump ring to attach the extension chain.
3. Use an 8mm jump ring to attach one charm to the center of the strand.
4. On one end of the pearl and silver link chain, attach three 8mm jump rings and a 12mm jump ring. Attach the 12mm jump ring to the 8mm jump ring on one end of the pearl and double-chain. Repeat for the remaining end of the chain.
5. For the pearl strand, use a 6mm silver jump ring to attach a small silver clasp to each end of the pearl necklace.
6. For the grey beaded chain, use a 6mm gunmetal jump ring to attach a gunmetal clasp to each end of the chain. Use a 6mm silver jump ring to attach the flower charm to the connector. Use an 8mm jump ring to attach the connector to the center of the chain. Leaving 2 beads in between, use 6mm jump rings to attach 2 charms on each side of the connector.
7. Attach the pearl strand and the grey beaded chain to the 12mm jump rings on the necklace.

Dreaming of Paris

Bag Charm

Use an 8mm jump ring to attach a lobster clasp to one end of a 5/8" length of chain. Use two 8mm jump rings to attach a cute camera pendant to the remaining end of the chain.

Earrings

For each earring, use a 4mm silver jump ring to attach a bead dangle to an ear wire. Our bead dangle included a faceted bead, rhinestone spacer, and pearl bead.

Bracelet

To make this blingy bracelet, attach one pearl and silver link double-chain piece (set aside from the necklace, page 24) to each end of an oval gemstone connector. Use a 6mm silver jump ring to attach a small lobster clasp to the chains on one end. Use a 6mm silver jump ring to attach a silver extension chain to the chains on the remaining end.

If pearls are not your thing, make it your own!

New York City

REVERSIBLE CIRCLE NECKLACE SHOPPING LIST

- ☐ two 1⁵/₈" diameter silver reversible circle pendants (rhinestones on one side, etched lines on opposite side) with attached chain tassels
- ☐ 36" long silver small and large circle chain
- ☐ 20" long silver medium link chain
- ☐ extension chain
- ☐ 12mm silver jump rings
- ☐ 6mm silver jump rings
- ☐ 3mm silver jump ring
- ☐ small silver lobster clasp
- ☐ chain-nose pliers (2 pair)

Finished necklace length: approximately 30"

Reversible Circle Necklace

1. Remove the tassels from the circle pendants. Set the tassels aside to make the earrings.
2. Separate the circle chain into the following pieces: two $4\frac{3}{4}$", one 5", one 8", and one 12".
3. Separate the medium link chain into the following pieces: two 1", one $6\frac{1}{4}$", and one 10".
4. Using a 6mm jump ring, attach the lobster clasp to one 1" length of medium chain. Attach the medium chain to one $4\frac{3}{4}$" length of circle chain. Using a 6mm and a 12mm jump ring, attach the circle chain to the loop on one circle pendant.
5. Using the 3mm jump ring, attach the extension chain to the remaining 1" length of medium chain. Attach the medium chain to the remaining $4\frac{3}{4}$" length of circle chain. Using a 6mm and a 12mm jump ring, attach the circle chain to the loop on the remaining circle pendant.
6. Attach five 12mm jump rings to each circle pendant.

For Steps 7-11, use 6mm jump rings to attach chain lengths to the 12mm jump rings.

7. Attach the 5" length of circle chain to the first set of jump rings (nearest the neck).
8. Attach the $6\frac{1}{4}$" length of medium chain to the second set of jump rings.
9. Attach the 8" length of circle chain to the third set of jump rings.
10. Attach the 10" length of medium chain to the fourth set of jump rings.
11. Attach the 12" length of circle chain to the fifth set of jump rings.

Tassel Earrings

Shimmery chain earrings are easy to make. Just remove any kind of decorative cover the tassels may have and add ear wires to the tassel tops.

New York City

BRACELET SHOPPING LIST

- ☐ three 1" diameter smooth silver rings
- ☐ three $^{7}/_{8}$" diameter hammered silver rings
- ☐ 8mm silver jump rings
- ☐ small silver lobster clasp
- ☐ chain-nose pliers (2 pair)

Finished bracelet length: approximately $7^{1}/_{2}$"

Bracelet

1. Alternating rings and using two jump rings together between each set of rings, join the large rings together.
2. Join two jump rings together end to end. Attach one jump ring to one bracelet end. Repeat for the remaining bracelet end. Attach the clasp to one bracelet end.

Circle Earrings

For each earring, use an 8mm silver jump ring to attach one 1" diameter smooth silver ring and one $^{7}/_{8}$" diameter hammered silver ring to an ear wire.

"LOVE" NECKLACE SHOPPING LIST

- ☐ 18" long silver medium chain with matching clasp and extension chain
- ☐ silver "Love" pendant (ours came on a key chain)
- ☐ 6mm silver jump rings
- ☐ chain-nose pliers (2 pair)

Finished necklace length: approximately 18"

Necklace

1. Separate the chain into two 7½" pieces (not including the clasp or extension chain).
2. Use jump rings to attach the chain ends to the pendant.

Thank you

for purchasing this book. In appreciation, Lena is offering a free mp3 music download. Follow the link below to go to her Pennies From Heaven Jewelry website and submit the code WANDER2016.

http://www.penniesfromheavenjewelry.com/#!wanderlust/c1cn

Production Team: Technical Writer – Lisa Lancaster; Technical Associate – Mary Sullivan Hutcheson; Editorial Writer – Susan Frantz Wiles; Senior Graphic Artist – Lora Puls; Graphic Artist – Cailen Cochran; Photostylist – Angela Alexander; and Photographer – Jason Masters.